CW0051700S

The Albatross

3RD & MAIN

by Simon David Eden

WWW.SAMUELFRENCH.CO.UK
WWW.SAMUELFRENCH.COM

FOR AMATEUR PRODUCTION ENQUIRIES

UNITED KINGDOM AND WORLD EXCLUDING NORTH AMERICA
plays@SamuelFrench-London.co.uk
020 7255 4302/01
UNITED STATES AND CANADA
info@SamuelFrench.com
1-866-598-8449
Each title is subject to availability from Samuel French, depending upon country of performance.

Shiny Pin Productions

present

The Albatross 3rd & Main

The Albatross 3rd & Main was first performed at Emporium Brighton on 2nd February 2016 with the following cast:

1st Cast & Company:

Lullaby	**GEOFF AYMER**
Gene	**NICHOLAS BOULTON**
Spider	**CHARLIE ALLEN**
Writer/Designer/Director	**SIMON DAVID EDEN**
Producer	**HELENA MICHELL**
Stage Manager	**SAMMI WOOLLARD**
Assistant Stage Manager	**AMY SUTTON**
Costumier	**NICOLA HOLTER**
Lighting Designer	**STRAT MASTORIS**
Technician	**JOSHUA CRISP**
Photographer	**DAVID MYERS**
Fight Director	**ROGER BARTLETT**
Construction	**LES DEAN**

The company would like to extend special thanks to:

Keith & Jenny Michell. Emporium's Artistic Director James Weisz, Theatre Manager and design guru Nathan Potter, Kate Wood, and all the front of house staff. Niall & Chris of Drive Wild Horses. Chris Wey of The Design Company (for the reclaimed timber!) Jeannie Brooke Barnett. Millie Eden, Matt Lipsey. And Treat Williams for being the best possible transatlantic sounding board!

Author's Note

Sam Shepard once remarked that not only did he not know what a play was about when he set about writing it, but often, he didn't know even after he'd finished. Now I can't say that of 'Albatross', but it is true that much of what found its way onto the page as I spent time with the characters, came from my sub-conscious. So what's a British writer doing writing an American stage play? Well, all artists reflect the times in which they create their work, and there's no doubt that the subtext of this satire - the repercussions of cultural imperialism - is to be found centre stage in our daily news bulletins. Throughout history, even the most powerful empires – The Persian, Roman, Caliphate, Mongol, Spanish, British etc. – were eventually surpassed and reaped what they had sown, only today, we get to observe every inch of that inevitable fall in the relative comfort of our living rooms, in wide-screen surround sound high definition.

But to take a step or two back...

I'm what you might call a research junkie, and the idea for the play grew out of several seemingly disparate discoveries made a few years apart. The first was that Samuel Taylor Coleridge (whose epic poem Rime of the Ancient Mariner inspired the Albatross of the title) had, in 1795, given a passionate lecture in Bristol on the barbarity of the slave trade. Nothing unusual in that you might say, for a liberal poet-philosopher of the times. But what struck me, is how deeply troubled Coleridge was by his own guilt by association, of living in a society, in a thriving major port that profited from mans inhumanity to man.

The second discovery concerned those iconic wooden sculptures of Native Americans. The so-called Cigar Store Indians, which gained huge popularity with storekeepers in the US in the 19th century. And these were not mere ornamentation, they encouraged commerce, and were used as a means to communicate to an illiterate customer base, that tobacco products were readily available on the premises where they stood. Born out of the early trade between settlers and the indigenous population – who were masters of cultivating the crop - these figures were often carved by artisans connected to the shipping industry seeking an outlet for their talents when the demand for figureheads for the bows of tall ships was in decline. Today some Native Americans consider the symbol an offensive reminder of a period in history in which the settler-colonists expropriated their tribal lands and began to eradicate their culture.

The third piece of the creative puzzle was a brief news article that caught my eye during my last visit to Vermont, New England. It concerned Federal legislation relating to the protection of the very symbol of the nation, the American eagle. Or more specifically, the golden eagle, a creature no longer listed on the endangered species list, yet one still protected by the letter of the law. This latter enshrined in the US Constitution, is the reason the tale is set, could only be set, in the United States of America.

Now quite why those three elements would fuse in my imagination and find their way into a fictional general store in Massachusetts I cannot begin to say. But, as a student of human nature, I'm frequently drawn back to the kind of environment that I grew up in, in which the salty cut and thrust of the language and behaviour of the working man pitting his wits against the system, can be closely observed: the workshop, the construction site, the wreckers yard, the cafe, the bookmakers, the billiard hall and so on.

Each of these is imbued with its own set of rules and traditions, and those who frequent them, do so to commune, to strike a deal, to earn a crust, to gamble, to rib one another, to escape. To measure, in short, their own sense of self worth against the next fellow. And nowhere in my experience, can one find sharper wits, and greater insights into the human condition.

Ernest Hemingway once said: 'The good parts of a book may be only something a writer is lucky enough to overhear.' In the case of The Albatross 3rd & Main, that's not true of the plot or dialogue, but it is true of the nature and attitude of the characters. This play is rooted in a gritty blue-collar reality then, but by the same token (certainly for the premiere production which I'm also designing and directing) it's also a slightly off-key, heightened, symbolic, neo-noir reality. And by that I mean as a playwright, I'm as influenced by the great abstract artists and photographers and film-makers (cinema was a vital touchstone for Tennessee Williams, so it's good enough for me), as I am by theatre. So, if 'Albatross' - as some have remarked - can be said to have a dash of a Jim Jarmusch or the Coen Brothers about it, you won't hear me complaining.

Simon David Eden, February 2016

'How smooth must be the language of the whites, when they can make right look like wrong, and wrong like right.'

Chief Sauk Black Hawk
Ma-Ka-Tai-Me-She-Kia-Kiak
Rock Island, Illinois, 1833
*(as dictated to Antoine Leclair
U.S. Interpreter)*

For Dick Ross
the storyteller's storyteller

CAST OF CHARACTERS

All east-coast American

LOUIS 'LULLABY' LEE (40S/50S – African-American)

Lullaby is Gene's right hand man, a friendship born out of their shared passion for long nights deep sea fishing. A heavy-set, ex semi-pro featherweight boxer, he might have been a genuine sporting contender but for the mob guys and family craziness surrounding him in his prime. An avid reader of periodicals, he has an almost photographic memory for facts and figures. That said, there's no denying he also took one too many blows to the frontal lobe during his time in the ring, and that has slightly scrambled his wires and left him with a mild form of OCD. Loyal, hardworking, genial, Lullaby is also prone to unpredictable outbursts and, well, let's say, eccentric behaviour.

GENE LACY (40S/50S - Caucasian)

A former lobster boat fisherman and proprietor of Lacy's General Store. Given how little Gene wanted from life – a fishing boat, the chance to make a living from the sea, and a cute warm body to share his bed whenever he made it back to dry land, his tilt at the American Dream has been shot to pieces by the time we meet him. Landlocked, ducking creditors and gambling debts, he has an ex-wife with very expensive tastes, a business barely treading water, and a sense that time is running out on his attempt to hold it all together.

RICK 'SPIDER' RAGNO (30S - Caucasian)

Spider is the slick, ne'er-do-well desperado, born and raised in small town USA, who flunked school and has never held down a proper job in his life. Strangely likeable despite his semi-redneck attitude, (maybe because he doesn't even realize he's a bigot), he gets by ducking and diving around the fringes of the hardcore criminal fraternity that he'd like to consider himself a part of. More bark than bite, Spider (his surname is the Italian word for spider) never really thinks beyond the moment, which is both a blessing and a curse: the upside is he doesn't ever feel he's failed in any way, the downside, he's destined to keep reliving the old adage: if you keep doing what you do the way you do it, you'll keep getting what you get. And for Spider, ultimately, that's gotta be a lengthy stretch behind bars.

SCENE

GENERAL STORE, MASSACHUSETTS NEW ENGLAND USA

TIME

THE FALL, PRESENT DAY

ACT I

General Store – Morning

Outside it's the 21st century, but this place has hardly changed a lick since the 1800s. Whatever else is on display, there's a life size cigar store Native American in pride of place. A chess set, two chairs and a stack of periodicals by a wood burning stove.

LULLABY *is stacking cartons of bug poison on a shelf.*

GENE *is behind the counter, old style rotary dial telephone in hand.*

LULLABY *(reading label)* Fighting a losing battle? Fighting. A losing. Battle.

GENE *(on the phone)* Press one to connect with…two for… existing customers press…

LULLABY You hear that Cap'n Gene?

GENE Press four to hear these options again –

LULLABY Fighting a losing battle. 'S printed right here side a the pack.

GENE I can't press any… I can't press any goddamn thing I'm on a dial phone.

LULLABY Fighting a losing battle.

GENE *(re the phone)* Don't have to tell me.

LULLABY *(reading label)* Arm yourself against woodlouse, termites, ants, roaches and other annoying pests with this unique, ready-to-use Bomb-D-Bug-Fog All-in-One Handy Treatment.

GENE *(into phone)* Hello? Hello? Hello?

LULLABY Just shake and tug the tab to activate –

GENE I swear to god, what is it with these sonsofbitches –

LULLABY Will remain one hundred percent effective for up to nine months –

GENE If you can't take the call, don't pick up the phone. You know. You pick up the phone then take the goddamn call –

LULLABY Ideal for crack and crevice treatments, the Bomb-D-Bug-Fog can be used both indoors and out.

GENE *(into phone; measured)* Well. At long last. A real live human being. Deepak. Is that right? Eastern Seaboard? No? Pacific Northwest? No. There's a surprise. Pretty sure you ain't bunked down in Topeka Kansas am I right? Look. Never mind –

(pause) What?

(pause) Chicago Hope? The TV show?

(pause) Too bad they canned the series huh –

(pause) I'm sure you will make a fine doctor some day Deepak. And you need a reference *(for)* your Green Card I'm first in line OK. OK. But lookit. Today, right now what we need to deal with –

(measured) I appreciate it's not your fault Deepak. No. I fully appreciate that. But here's the thing. These debts I keep getting calls about. These debts you people keep harassing me about. These debts are not mine. They are not mine you un'erstand Deepak. And this must end here. Today. Right now.

(starting to ruffle) Would I mind holding? Would I *mind* holding? I've been holding. I just got through holding.

Yes I mind holding. I resent the fuck out of holding as a matter of fact –

LULLABY *heads out back for more supplies.*

(trying not to lose it) Don't, don't, don't, just hear me… don't… Deepak I swear to… Authorized payments? Yes it is a… Was. Was a *joint account* but…no I'm not interested in hearing details a debt repayment plan Deepak. I have no debt. I'm a debt free zone.

(pause) Yes I'm aware there's a forest a bounced checks. Yes I know about the lease on the Lexus GS, the maxed out Amex and Fidelity too. Ironic that don't you think the *Fidelity* card. What's that? Maxed out? It's an expression means…look. Lookit. Deepak. I'd love to spend the whole morning chewing the cud. Really I would. But…

(pause) We may have been Deepak. We may still have been man and wife at the time but –

(pause) Thirty. Thousand. Dollars. Let me…let me just dig around in my pockets here, take a look the cookie jar under the bed…well what do you know. I don't have thirty thousand dollars Deepak! I don't have it. I don't have it and if I did I wouldn't toss it into the hellfire that bitch warms her fanny by anyhow.

LULLABY *returns with more bug poison and continues to read the details on the pack.*

(pause) Re-establish the trust? Re-establish the trust? Is this what they teach you… This an intervention? You a marriage guidance counselor now? There was no trust the first place Deepak. That's the whole point. There was no trust. Now there is no union in the eyes a the law. And there is no debt I'm liable for you un'erstand me.

(losing it) What's that? No. No. Don't…do not transfer me! Stay on the line. Stay on the line. Stay on the line

Deepak. You. You. No you... YOU ...anymore a this harassment and I shall file suit –

LULLABY Smoke 'em out a doors, windows, porches and screens. Eaves, patios and stairways –

GENE *(into phone)* Email? Did you just say email? Well why didn't you say so before. I'll have my footman hop to it soon as he's Simonized my Jag-whar –

LULLABY ...log stores, attics and playsets –

SPIDER enters carrying a large cardboard box which he sets down on the counter.

GENE *(into phone)* Responsibility?

(pause) RESPONSIBILITY. What? What? If you...if you came into my store and a...and a...and a Mason jar of... of pickled beets fell off the shelf smacked you upside the head, you'd be looking to me for compensation am I right? Am I right? You'd be giving ME grief. Right? Right? Not the soda-lime glass manufacturer, not the beet farmer, not the guy cranks out the steel-pressed screw top lids.

(pause) What's a Mason jar?

(pause) No. Do not put me on hol –

Seeing that GENE is wound up, SPIDER makes for the coffee pot on the stove in back.

SPIDER (to **LULLABY**) Hey Champ.

SPIDER engages in a little mock sparring. LULLABY doesn't respond in kind, he just gives SPIDER a look and continues with his train of thought.

LULLABY ...barns, lean-tos, driveways and crawl spaces and other locations where pesky pests like to hide.

SPIDER Say what?

LULLABY Other locations where pesky pests like to hide?

> **SPIDER** *pours himself a coffee.*

SPIDER Porches –

LULLABY Said that

SPIDER Patios –

LULLABY Said that –

SPIDER Eaves –

LULLABY Said that –

SPIDER Upholstery.

LULLABY Upholstery? You think?

SPIDER What is this *Wheel of Fortune?*

LULLABY What say you Cap'n Gene?

GENE What?

LULLABY Other locations where pesky pests like to hide?

GENE Other locations where pesky pests like to hide? I'll tell you other locations where pesky pests like to hide.

> *(into phone)* IN GODDAMN DEBT COLLECTION CALL CENTERS IS WHERE THEY LIKE TO HIDE. AT THE OTHER END OF THIS DUMBASS PHONE IS WHERE THEY LIKE TO HIDE. And you can play that shitty middle-of-the-road *escalator* music all you want! I KNOW YOU CAN HEAR ME! I KNOW YOU CAN HEAR ME MISTER-CALLS-MAY-BE-RECORDED-FOR-TRAINING PURPOSES. WELL RECORD THIS OK! I – Deepak?
>
> *(reins in his temper)* No I'm not mad at you personally, though you did put me on hold again when I specifically requested you not do that. But hey, you're just doing your job right. I 'ppreciate that. They're paying you what, a buck an hour to work in a shithole white collar outsourcing sweatshop middle a fuckin' nowhere New

Delhi. You're mailing rupees back home to your family in the boonies. That's commendable. Really it is my friend. But don't let the schemin' leeches fool ya.

(picks up a magazine)

You get the National Geo-graphic your neck of the woods Deepak? Huh? The magazine. No. Well listen to this. What I'm going to tell you now, commit it to memory. Learn it by rote. Burn it into the back of your eye sockets. Those reruns a *Little House on the Prairie* in the tinpot Punjab branch of Bucket-O-Burger, that ain't cultural assimilation. It ain't. It just ain't. Now I want you to share this with your friends and family and all those you hold dear. You ready? You ready? Here it is:

(reading) A passionate attachment of one nation for another produces a variety of evils. Sympathy for the favored nation, facilitating the illusion of an imaginary common interest, in cases where no real common interest exists.

You get that? Huh. You get all that?

SPIDER *settles in a chair and buffs his cowboy boots with a cloth.*

(into phone) An illusion of an imaginary common interest, where no real common interest exists. You know who said that Deepak? Huh? You know who said that? George Washington is who. Seventeen nine'y six. George fuckin' Washington!

SPIDER   *(amused)* George Washington.

GENE   Now you can work the phone 'til you're blue in the face my friend, you can hound poor schmucks like me to their graves fifteen thousand miles away other side a the world, but you ain't never gonna walk in my shoes. Nor I yours.

SPIDER   Prob'ly don't even own a pair shoes.

GENE My point Deepak. The thrust of my dissertation here, is how YOU gonna help ME you don't even know where I live?

(pause) Not the address! I know you got the goddamn address! It's a figure of spee – He put me on hold! He put me on fuckin' hold!

GENE *looks around for something to act as a perfect payoff, the perfect punctuation. He comes up short, so instead, he slams the phone into its cradle, again and again and again.*

YOU GETTING THAT? HUH?! YOU GETTING THAT FOR TRAINING PURPOSES?! YOU GETTING THAT IN 3.D STEREO WRAP-AROUND HIGH DEFINITION TECHNICOLOR YOU BLOODSUCKING MOTHERFUCKERS!

GENE *slams the phone down one final time.*

Debt repayment plans. Bridging loans. Life insurance. Who are these fuckin' people. Hah! What life? What life do I need insurance for? Deepak's making out better'n I am.

Pause.

SPIDER Good morning Gene.

GENE *(still smoldering)* Looking forward to the goddamn day I don't have to draw breath in this stinking hellhole.

SPIDER You want some coffee?

SPIDER *picks up the National Geographic and flips through.* **LULLABY** *crosses and takes it from him.*

GENE Would I mind holding? Would I mind holding? Where does he get off? I mean either fish or chop bait!

SPIDER You know they say that anger is a problem-solving emotion.

LULLABY Who says that?

SPIDER Talkin' to Gene.

(to **GENE***)* They say it gives us energy and motivates us to act.

LULLABY Motivates us? Motivates us how?

SPIDER Talkin' to Gene.

(to **GENE***)* But intense unresolved anger…well you just don't wanna go down that road.

LULLABY You don't?

SPIDER No you don't. You know why?

LULLABY 'Cause it's unresolved?

SPIDER 'Cause it's the sure fire way to drive a nail into your own coffin. It's gonna eat away at your insides just like the worse kind a disease. We're talkin' high blood pressure, anxiety, coronary whatnot, co-less-stral off the chart –

LULLABY Cholesterol? Just from being mad –

SPIDER Talkin' to Gene.

(to **GENE***)* But if you harness that sucker. You harness that rage…that simmering resentment…that balls out, fuck you, I will not take it anymore attitude. Well, then life is the grit in your fat juicy oyster my friend. 'Fore you know it, you've ground yourself a pearl.

LULLABY *(re the box)* UPS been and gone.

SPIDER That right?

LULLABY Pickup's 'fore eight thirty, A of the M, Tuesdays and Thursdays.

SPIDER UPS. Forget UPS. I'm talking 'bout potential –

LULLABY Potential?

SPIDER Potent…shall. Potent…shale. I'm talking mining the bedrock of your very being. I'm talking jacking, big dog fracking, blazing like a forest fire and yes we can the can!

Pause.

GENE You keep on puffing Smokey Bear.

SPIDER Only thing smoked is in that there box. And that's *elevator* music. Not *escalator* music.

GENE Say what?

SPIDER Like you said before. I mean it was sweet, don't get me wrong. But it's the finer details. I got an ear these things you know. Never miss a beat.

GENE You got an ear?

SPIDER Yessir I do.

GENE Van-fucking-Gogh.

SPIDER Better believe it.

GENE You gonna paint me a picture Vincent?

SPIDER Oh this is my masterpiece. This is my signature work. This is the one you gonna remember me for.

GENE Fuck you talkin' about?

SPIDER *(to* **LULLABY** *re his coffee)* This freshly brewed?

LULLABY What day is it?

SPIDER What day is it? Thursday. What day is it.

GENE Then it's freshly brewed. From Monday.

> **LULLABY** *enjoys the joke.*

SPIDER Jocularity. Mirth. Truly, my sides are splitting. But you know, I worry about you Gene I really do.

GENE That's touching.

SPIDER You may jest, but I kid you not.

GENE Well that's something for my tombstone.

SPIDER No seriously. I come in here, what every other day the last what ten years –

GENE Every other day –

SPIDER Every other week anyways and I see you –

GENE I'm right here –

SPIDER And you're just –

GENE Putting in a shift –

SPIDER You're just –

GENE Open for business –

SPIDER I'm sorry to say it –

GENE You're sorry to say it? You didn't say anything.

SPIDER You've weighed anchor and you're treading water my friend. You're dead in the water and you don't even know it. That's what I'm saying.

GENE That's what you're saying?

SPIDER That's what I'm saying. Been floatin' 'round here so long you got barnacles 'stead a balls. You're taking on water Gene, I know it, you know it, Father Time, well he sure as hell knows it.

GENE But now you gonna throw me a lifesaver, is that what you're saying Spider?

SPIDER You know what I'm saying.

GENE *I* know what you're saying? *I* know what you're saying? Even *you* don't know what you're saying half the time.

SPIDER You might think different when you see what I brung gift wrapped and set in your lap today.

LULLABY UPS has already dispatched.

SPIDER You said that.

LULLABY Pickup is 'fore eight thirty. Eight thirty on the button. Man's already been and gone.

SPIDER Man's already been and gone.

LULLABY You best believe it.

SPIDER *(pause)* Well we can all take comfort in that don't you think. It's a beautiful thing. The wheels of commerce and industry well greased and grinding on, rumbling right on past our windows we sleep sound at night, tucked up tight as bugs in a rug.

LULLABY Bugs in a rug?

SPIDER Say what?

LULLABY That's it. Bugs in rugs.

SPIDER Are you on any heavy meds?

LULLABY Other locations where pesky pests like to hide –

SPIDER ...'cause you should be.

LULLABY Arm yourself against woodlouse, termites, ants, roaches and other annoying pests with this unique, ready-to-use Bomb-D-Bug-Fog All-in-One Handy Treatment...

SPIDER *(to GENE)* A word in your shell-like.

GENE Shoot.

LULLABY Just shake and tug the tab to activate. Will remain one hun'red per cent effective for up to nine whole months –

SPIDER Does he have to... I mean this is *business*...a business thing so...

LULLABY Ideal for crack and crevice treatments –

SPIDER Gotta love a crack and a crevice –

LULLABY Bomb-D-Bug can be used both indoors and out –

SPIDER *(to* **GENE***)* A word in *private*. Maybe there are errands –

GENE Errands?

SPIDER You know, for…you know…so we can talk. Matters concerning. We can speak of things.

GENE Speak of things?

SPIDER Openly…candidly. Business. Cramping my style.

GENE Right.

> *(to* **LULLABY***)* Hey boss. Mister Ragno here wants to speak openly and candidly about some business. Are you OK with that?

LULLABY Business?

GENE So he claims.

LULLABY Openly and candidly?

GENE Seems to be the play.

LULLABY Fine by me.

SPIDER Boss?

GENE You should drop in a little more Spider. I signed over the whole kit and caboodle to Louis a good three months back. I work for him now.

SPIDER *(a moment to consider)* Get the fuck out.

GENE I got the fuck out.

SPIDER Then why the fuck you still here?

GENE Where would I go?

SPIDER You…?

> *(pause)* Wait a second here. You…? What the fuck? What the fuck is that? You get out but you stay in?

GENE Free country.

SPIDER Oh I get it. Yeah. Yeah. Yeah.

GENE What? You get what?

SPIDER Yeah it's like that whaddaya call it...where the hostage falls for the hostage taker. The victim falls for the perp. You know, empathy and shit. Stockhausen Syndrome.

GENE You're saying I fell for Louis?

SPIDER Not in the...no. No, no, no, not in the biblical sense.

   (pause) Did you?

GENE Hey Lou. You soft on me. You want we should swing hands? Grab a soda catch a movie later?

LULLABY They say blonds are more fun...but I'm gonna pass.

GENE But we'll always have Paris right.

LULLABY *Quelle belle journée!*

GENE Like he said.

SPIDER Cute. Dean Martin and Jerry Screwloose.

LULLABY *(to SPIDER)* And that's <u>Stockholm</u> Syndrome.

SPIDER Huh?

LULLABY *(pointed)* <u>Stockholm</u> Syndrome.

SPIDER 'S what I said.

LULLABY You said Stockhausen.

SPIDER Did I fuck.

LULLABY He's a fella makes music and such –

SPIDER I know what I said OK. Jeez. What? What? You think 'cause you're the big cheese now that makes you Einstein all of a sudden. Guy slips a noose around your neck, fuckin' cross to bear with this backwoods piece a shit craphouse an' you think you're all made up?

(to GENE*)* I mean no offense.

GENE Oh none taken.

SPIDER *(to* LULLABY*)* I mean fuck you you know. You don't know shit from Shinola, ass from your elbow. Maybe you pay a little more attention you might actually learn something about something don't come from the back a no tub a Deet or a TV show.

GENE 'S okay Lullaby. Don't pay him no mind. Spider just needs a little more fiber *(in)* his diet.

LULLABY *exits out back with the empty carton.*

Hey go easy OK. Lou's a sensitive guy.

SPIDER Sensitive? Sensitive. Well excuse me Doc, but what the fuck? I mean are you serious? You just gave him the whole operation lock, stock and barrel?

GENE Lock, stock, barrel and the Bomb-D-Bug.

SPIDER Is this like a handshake kinda deal? I mean you didn't draw up papers nothin'. You didn't 'Call Saul'.

GENE His evil twin anyways.

SPIDER Signed, sealed, delivered I'm yours?

GENE In triplicado.

SPIDER *(disappointed)* Gene. Gene. Gene. Gene. Gene.

GENE Ricky. Ricky. Ricky. Ricky. Ricky.

SPIDER And what about me?

GENE What about you?

SPIDER Now that hurts Gene. I got my sensitivities too you know and we go back a ways. Quite a ways. So I figure if you're just going to…to piss your worldly goods up a wall and be done with your material possessions, right thing to do, might have been to sequester a little aside for me.

GENE You figure.

SPIDER I do. I mean I'm pleased for Rain Man there. I am.

GENE I know you are. And don't call him that.

SPIDER What?

GENE Rain Man.

SPIDER If I have cast aspersions and caused offense then I am truly sorry.

GENE He's not whatdoyoucallit…when they got the thing. Counting tooth picks. Scrubbing their hands every five minutes. Cussing for no good reason –

SPIDER Artistic.

GENE Right. He's just punchy. One too many haymakers to the frontal lobe. One minute he's lucid –

SPIDER *(enjoying it)* The next he's humping garbage cans –

GENE Fuck you Rick. Louis was a helluva fine fighter his day.

SPIDER Don't dispute it.

GENE Shoulda had a shot the featherweight title –

SPIDER Ronald McDonald put paid to that though right. Super size me baby!

GENE Hey. Ex-fighters have a tendency to balloon.

SPIDER To balloon?

GENE Sure. You take Jake LaMotta or Big John Tate –

SPIDER OK. So they balloon.

GENE Just go easy.

SPIDER Easy. Go easy. Sure. Fine by me. Easy pickings, easy
street. All I'm saying, it's like they say: we are what we
do.

GENE We are what we do? Is that what they say?

SPIDER We are what we do.

GENE I thought they say: we are what we eat.

SPIDER Well…they say a lot of things –

GENE Yes they do –

SPIDER But it's action talks louder than words you know.
That's what I'm saying. And that's what I stand by as
I live and breathe. You do what you do and you get
judged accordingly. You go out on a limb, you don't go
out on a limb, on your head be it.

GENE The limb?

SPIDER The consequence. Now don't poke fun Gene I'm
serious here.

GENE I can see that you are.

SPIDER I came here today because I thought we was
friends.

GENE Friends –

SPIDER Buddies. Running mates. Brothers in arms.
Because that to me…that to me is the thing makes
this world turn on its axis. We are none of us tropical
islands you know. Man is not designed to be in and of
himself alone. Adrift. Adrift from all others. Floating
in some dark lonely sea of isolation. You hear what I'm
saying?

GENE I do and I think it's admirable.

SPIDER Well thank you.

GENE You are more than welcome. But this ship and all
that sails in her –

SPIDER Yeah?

GENE That belongs to Lullaby.

SPIDER Did I say otherwise? Man makes arrangements to offload some creditors, who am I to point a finger.

GENE What?

SPIDER I mean what with your ex-old lady carrying on like she's Mrs Trump the third and the IRS am I right. Am I right. You got repo man breathing down your neck so you offload to Simple Simon here, you hand the bat-on to big Lennie-tell-me-about-the-rabbits 'fore you get the knock on the door. That is wily I will grant you. They can't take what you don't own right. Am I right?

GENE The IRS? The IRS ain't got nothing to do with nothin'. Place is a going concern.

SPIDER A going concern –

GENE Just I ain't concerned about where it's going.

SPIDER To hell in a hand basket you ask me.

GENE Look. Granted, ain't nobody gonna get rich propping up this here counter. And that angel of mercy I was hitched to for five minutes, she did clean me out. But the mortgage is done and dusted. Place ticks over. Just time for some new blood is all.

SPIDER (*pause*) New blood? Lullaby's been here so long he's part of the fixtures and fittings.

GENE I sell it on, get the hell out of Dodge, what's he gonna do? Answer me that. He's got a home-sweet-home sign hanging on the crib barn door for crying out loud.

SPIDER Well there you go. You see that's what I'm saying. We stick together. Strength in numbers. All hands to the pump. That's what sets us apart from the animals.

GENE That and the flush John.

> **LULLABY** *returns with the empty carton and returns to the shelf of Bomb-D-Bug.*

All peachy there Chief?

LULLABY All peachy Cap'n Gene.

> **LULLABY** *begins to empty the shelf of the Bomb-D-Bug, putting it back in the carton.*

SPIDER Hey Louis. Didn't you just stack them shelves?

GENE Spider –

SPIDER I mean did you not just pop that Bomb-D-Bug right on that shelf not two ticks of a lambs tail ago.

GENE Ricky I won't say it sweet again –

SPIDER I mean you know you did that right?

LULLABY 'Course I know I did done and do it. I ain't slow.

SPIDER I know you're just punchy.

LULLABY Had me a change a heart.

SPIDER What's that?

LULLABY Don't know if I wanna be sellin' wares that killin' critters.

SPIDER *(to GENE)* You hearing this.

GENE 'S his store. Guess he can sell what he wants.

> *There's a sound off. The crash of something heavy falling.*

LULLABY Cap'n Gene?

GENE Don't sweat it Lou. Just the raccoon rumba – he'll be dancin' in the dumpster again.

GENE *exits out back.* SPIDER *tops up his coffee. For a moment he watches* LULLABY *removing the stock from the shelves. During the following passage,* LULLABY *moves to the chess board and studies it. A game is in progress,* LULLABY *playing himself. (He makes no more than two moves in the whole first Act)*

SPIDER You know Lullaby, you quit selling stuff that kills stuff, you might as well draw the blinds hang up the gone fishing sign now. Coffee, tobaccy, candy, every damn thing in this store oughta be sold with a health warning. Not that I don't admire your sense of civic duty. I myself often lie awake in the wee small hours wondering about the plight of those less fortunate than our good selves. The lower orders so to speak. But first off it's a man's duty to see that he has his own house in order. Can't help others you can't help yourself. You see what I'm saying. You follow? Now you take this store here. Now I know that Gene, he's a good man, he's a man a principle, and I know that he sees qualities in you that…well…legacy is not too strong a word I would venture. He's put a lot of his best years into this place –

LULLABY Done sold his lobster boat to buy it –

SPIDER Yes he did. And he's a proud man –

LULLABY You lost at sea, Cap'n Gene's the man you want in the wheelhouse –

SPIDER All in favor say aye.

LULLABY Aye –

SPIDER And now Cap'n Gene believes you're the man fit to take the bridge. And I do too. I do. But I just want you to know, that if ever, at any time of the day or night, if you ever feel that burden is too heavy to bear alone, you having trouble finding your sea-legs, I want you to know you can rely on me. Call on me. You un'erstand Lullaby? You un'erstand what I'm saying here? You need a first mate, someone to help navigate this ship, negotiate them choppy waters ahead, then you look no further than ol' Ricardo. This is just 'tween you and me, you un'erstand. But I'm with you on this you need me skipper. What you think about that?

LULLABY *(pause)* The ant's a fine beast. Smart too. Smarter than some folks I know.

SPIDER Ants?

LULLABY Formicidae to give them theys proper name.

SPIDER Ants are smart?

LULLABY Real smart.

SPIDER You think so?

LULLABY I know so. They's highly evolved.

SPIDER Highly evolved huh. You know what I think. I think you oughta get yourself a bigger hat; band's too tight Louis, you ain't gettin' enough oxygen to your brain cells. I mean you ever see an ant behind the wheel of a Cadillac coupé? Or running for governor, how about that? Hell you ever seen an ant could even swim worth a damn?

LULLABY They's what's known as a super-organism.

SPIDER A super-organism?

LULLABY They got a hierarchy. A whole chain of command. They got queens and workers and soldiers and they farm too.

SPIDER They farm?

LULLABY Sure do. They farm aphids –

SPIDER Where d'you get all this shit?

LULLABY Periodicals.

SPIDER Periodicals.

LULLABY And you know they do not work for personal benefit, but only to benefit the colony as a whole. They don't see themselves as individuals. They see themselves as part of something bigger. A family. And so when they find themselves a tasty meal, a sugary treat –

SPIDER They share it with their pals –

LULLABY Yes they do. But that's not the super smart part –

SPIDER It's not?

LULLABY Uh-uh. The super smart part is even though they've just found a plentiful supply a nourishment, even though there's enough food to go round for everyone, couple of those little critters will right away begin to strategise –

SPIDER Strategise?

LULLABY That's right. Theys think ahead. Always lookin out for tomorrow. What's around the corner.

SPIDER How d'you mean exactly?

LULLABY They'll be munchin' away *(on)* some grub, some honeydew or whatever, and a couple of 'em, they'll peel away while the going's still good, lit out in search of the next meal. The next treasure trove. The next nutritious bounty so to speak.

SPIDER So to speak.

LULLABY And that's 'fore they even need it. 'Fore theys buddies is sitting around with empty bellies, scratching their heads saying boy I sure could use me a snack. And who's gonna tell the queen the cupboard is bare?!

SPIDER Well now you is talkin' Louis. You know…you're on to something there my man. You're on to something there. That's enterprising. And that's exactly what I been trying to tell ol' Gene.

GENE *returns.*

GENE Tell ol' Gene what?

LULLABY Raccoon?

GENE Uh-hu. Fish bones in the garbage. But tell ol' Gene what?

SPIDER Enterprise. Opportunity. You gotta take a leaf out of ol' Lullaby's book. I can see why you made him your heir apparent. He's right switched on. Him and his ants. All for one and one for all. Tell him Louis. Tell Gene here about the super-organism.

LULLABY They's a super-organism.

GENE I don't doubt it, but I should know this because?

SPIDER Because we are those ants. You, me, Lullaby. There's food on the table. A roof above our heads. But though our nests are feathered we still gots to feather the nest.

GENE Ants, tables, feathers, what the fuck are you talking about Spider? Have you been sucking on the weed again?

SPIDER I have two words for you –

GENE Yeah? And I've got two for you: go fuck yourself.

LULLABY That's three words.

GENE There's a silent 's'.

Pause.

SPIDER Take a look in that there box.

GENE Why so?

SPIDER Take a perusal.

GENE What's in there Spider?

SPIDER Well take a looksee.

LULLABY I'll take a looksee.

GENE 'S your store Lullaby, you can do whatever you please.

LULLABY moves to the box. He considers SPIDER and GENE.

LULLABY 'S like Santy Claus came early.

As LULLABY opens the flaps and peers into the box he reels from the smell.

(pause) Is that what I think it is?

SPIDER I don't know Louis, what do you think it is?

LULLABY Well it's a bit squished in the box an' all –

SPIDER Yeah but so –

LULLABY Well I'd say... I'd say...

SPIDER You'd say what?

LULLABY I'd say that was a Rhode Island Red rooster.

SPIDER *(pause)* A Rhode Island Red...?!

GENE A chicken?

SPIDER And you gave this bufflehead the goddamn keys to the castle!

GENE You're shipping a cock a doodle-do? Why you shippin' a cock a doodle-do?

LULLABY UPS has been and gone –

SPIDER I ain't shipping nothin'! And that ain't no goddamn poultry. That's a golden fuckin' eagle man! A golden fuckin' eagle!

LULLABY That's four words.

SPIDER Yeah? Well fuckin' sue me OK.

GENE looks in the box.

GENE A golden eagle? You sure that's a golden eagle?

SPIDER 'Less the Pentagon's breeding Bantams, sure I'm sure.

LULLABY Why's it smell so bad?

SPIDER You ever seen one up close before.

LULLABY No.

SPIDER 'Course not. Not too many have. So that's what they smell like.

They all peer into the box.

GENE Fucker stinks.

LULLABY Maybe it's fear you know. Pheromones. Moment a death. Used to smell it in the ring time to time.

SPIDER That's a good point Louis. You may have something there.

GENE Big motherfucker.

SPIDER You're talking a bird a prey will hunt a wolf.

LULLABY I've heard that.

SPIDER You heard right.

GENE That's <u>a lot</u> of bird.

SPIDER Pound for pound gives Charlie Parker a run for his moolah.

GENE So where d'you find this thing anyways?

SPIDER Tweety Pie found me. I'm minding my own business, noodling on down the highway. Boz Scaggs on the FM. Sonofabitch flew right on into the windshield. *WHUMP!*

GENE Boz Scaggs. 'Lowdown'?

SPIDER 'Loan Me a Dime'.

LULLABY Boz and the Sky Dog. Sweet.

GENE So you're cruisin' –

SPIDER Fucker drops out of the big blue bounces right off the glass. Scared the bejeezus outta me. Thought I was back in A-raq.

GENE A-raq? You was never in A-raq. You was never in the military.

SPIDER Hey man I enlisted you know. Is it my fault they wanted a high school diploma and college credits.

GENE I'm thinking 'repeat offender' didn't look so good on the application neither.

> **GENE** *and* **LULLABY** *enjoy the retort.*

SPIDER Fuck that. It's about the comradery you know. The spirit. I was there with our boys. You didn't need to be there to be there, you know what I'm saying.

LULLABY So it's dead right?

SPIDER What?

LULLABY The golden eagle.

SPIDER What do you think?

GENE So what's your plan?

SPIDER My plan?

GENE What, today is show and tell. You brung a box a ripe roadkill into class?

SPIDER You wanna know what my plan is? Here's my plan. We make like Lullaby's ants. We get ants in our pants.

GENE What?

SPIDER You pick up the phone.

GENE I pick up the phone?

SPIDER You pick up the phone and call your man on the res.

GENE My man on the res?

SPIDER The res, you know, the res, the Mohawk reservation over in Franklin County.

LULLABY The Kahniakenhaka. That's what the Mohawks call Mohawks.

GENE I call the reservation?

SPIDER That's what I'm saying.

GENE And why would I do that?

SPIDER Because you got an in there. Jeez do I have to spell it out.

GENE Yeah. Yeah I think maybe you do Ricky. I think maybe you should spell it out line by line word for word.

SPIDER Well all right then –

GENE I'm all ears –

SPIDER Join the dots –

GENE Bated breath –

SPIDER Who's your man over there again?

GENE My man?

SPIDER Your in?

GENE Waneek. She's my man over there.

SPIDER She?

GENE 'S right.

SPIDER A broad?

GENE That's right.

SPIDER Huh. I din know that.

GENE Well you learn somethin' new every day.

SPIDER Well well, Cap'n Gene Lacy in a whole new light. You like a little feral tail okay. I'm down with that desperado. Little wig wam bam –

GENE She's a healer.

SPIDER A healer?

GENE That's what I said.

SPIDER You mean like a medicine man?

GENE Waneek is a tribal elder.

LULLABY Waneek means 'One who keeps the Peace'.

SPIDER That a fact? Well this is all upside my friends.

GENE How so?

SPIDER Get Pocahontas on the line. She'll tell ya. Our late feathered friend in the box here. This baby'll fetch a king's fuckin' ransom. D'you know how many people there are on the waiting list?

GENE What waiting list?

SPIDER For a juvenile golden eagle – that's the hot ticket – we're talkin' six figures. There's a five year waiting list. FIVE FUCKIN' YEARS. You got braves the length and breadth of the USA pacing their teepees like junkies waitin' a fix. Pow-wows, ceremonies shit, this is an essential item, an essential item, and they are climbing the animal hide walls man. They are bouncing off the mud huts walls. Can't get their grubby mitts on 'em. And you know why? You know why? 'Cause only enrolled members of Federally approved tribes get to sup from the *white mans'* well.

  (to LULLABY*)* No offense Louis.

LULLABY Oh none taken.

SPIDER US Fish and Wildlife Service got the whole operation sowed up tight. 'S a license to print money is what it is. Created their own black market. Every time a bird drops off its perch, goes tits up: ker-fuckin-ching. Cochise gonna pay through the bone in his nose.

GENE A waiting list huh?

SPIDER 'S why I advocate divide and conquer.

GENE Divide and –?

SPIDER Slice and dice. Cold cuts. A wing here, a talon there, a beak, a skull – and shake that sweet sweet tail feather baby. Feathers alone worth a small fortune.

GENE Is that a fact?

SPIDER Yes it is. And I think it's our duty as good citizens to do our bit for the plight of the indigenous of this fine nation. These eagles are the very lifeblood of their beliefs. No tribal dance, celebration or ceremony is complete without their presence. There's bare knuckle fights break out over a plume. A plume I kid you not. And here we are in possession of a fully plumed goldmine.

LULLABY But it's illegal.

SPIDER 'S that Lullaby?

LULLABY Talkin' to Cap'n Gene.

SPIDER Talkin' to Cap'n Gene?

LULLABY Talkin' to Cap'n Gene.

SPIDER Look this don't concern you okay. I'm conducting a private conversation over here and I'd appreciate a little…just stack your shelves OK. I mean sweep the porch whatever. 'S your porch now right. Right. Your wares. Your store. So mind your store and mind your own fuckin' business while you're at it. OK. OK. OK.

GENE What say Louis?

LULLABY The bird. The eagle. It's a felony offense. Right up there with robbery, larceny, homicide –

GENE A felony? To what, to sell a dead bird?

LULLABY Even to let it lie there.

SPIDER Where d'you get that?

LULLABY A periodical.

SPIDER A periodical?

LULLABY I read me an article.

SPIDER Oh you read you an article.
Well whoopseefuckindoo –

LULLABY And there was that fella over in Belchertown, got busted for hawkin' a fan made a eagle feathers on the Inter-web.

GENE A fan?

LULLABY Like a ladies' fan. One thousand dollars he was askin'. He done got jail time.

GENE You're saying I could be incarcerated –

LULLABY And land a fine –

GENE A fine?

LULLABY I don't recollect entirely, but a hun'red, two hun'red thousand g's –

GENE TWO HUNDRED THOU ...from just having a box a road-kill on my counter?!

LULLABY 'S my counter Cap'n Gene. 'S my counter now.

GENE *(to SPIDER)* Get that fucking thing outta here. I ain't doing jail time on this Rick. No way I'm going *(to)* the pen for goddamn cold cuts.

SPIDER Will you relax.

GENE No. No I will not relax. Get that fuckin' stiff outta here!

GENE *lifts the box and shoves it into* SPIDER*'s arms.*

Go! Now! Get the fuck out!

SPIDER *(pause)* I can't.

GENE Why not?

SPIDER Bird's heavy.

GENE Carried it in didn't ya.

SPIDER But I got no means a transportation.

GENE What?

SPIDER Kaylee-Sue took the rambler.

GENE Kaylee-Sue.

SPIDER Dropped me off.

GENE Who the fuck is Kaylee-Sue?

SPIDER *sets the box back on the counter.*

LULLABY Don't be putting that *(on)* my counter.

GENE Who the fuck is Kaylee-Sue? She know about this?

SPIDER No. No. I was on my way to pick her up when this
fucker slammed into me. You should see her Gene.
One hundred and twenty pounds a peaches and cream
–

GENE Great. That special someone to keep in mind, *(when)*
you're jerking off in Folsom.

SPIDER Don't be that way Gene. We can work this out.

GENE Oh you think?

SPIDER Naturally. 'S why I came here? I got the goods, you
got the in. All you got to do is make one call. One call
and we's partners. Fifty fifty down the line.

LULLABY 'S my store. How come I ain't a party?

GENE Oh you're a party all right Louis, you're an accessory before the fact just like me.

LULLABY Just 'cause we looked in the box?

GENE Just 'cause we looked in the box.

SPIDER Accessory before the...you know you watch too much TV.

GENE Maybe you don't watch enough.

SPIDER One lousy call Gene. One lousy call. Don't look this gift horse in the mouth.

GENE Gift horse. A fuckin' <u>albatross</u> is what it is?

LULLABY Ah! Well a-day! What evil looks had I from old and young! Instead of the cross, the albatross about my neck was hung.

GENE *and* **SPIDER** *consider* **LULLABY**.

My gran'pa used to read me that poem. You know it Cap'n Gene: 'The Rime the Ancient Mariner'.

(transported) How in days a yore a sailor killed a giant seabird. Brought every last man on his ship bad luck. Crew made him wear the maggoty corpse around his neck as a penance. Then Death and the Nightmare Life-in-Death play dice to damn their souls all to hell! 'Cepting the Mariner. He was forced to live out his days walkin' the Earth a ghost of hisself retelling the grim and grisly tale.

Long pause.

SPIDER *(to* **GENE***)* So you gonna make the call or what?

GENE Just slow the fuck on down there Spider. Jus' slow the fuck on down. You waltz in here jus' 'specting I'd make the call?

SPIDER First among equals Gene. First among equals.

GENE *(pause)* What the fuck does that even mean?

SPIDER Means it weren't no decision taken lightly.

GENE There's a load off.

SPIDER Guess I hold you in higher esteem than you do yourself.

GENE What?

SPIDER You un'er estimate your own potential Gene. I seen it a million times. And I get it, you know. It's the way society is. Makes us feel like we got to conform. Fit in. Run with the crowd. Swim with the tide. But I say the hell with that.

GENE You do.

SPIDER I do. However the cookie crumbles. However the runes may fall you know.

GENE Runes? Did you say runes?

SPIDER Now you take Kaylee-Lee. She's a Pisces. And it's true they are prone to substance abuse on account a their eternal search for themselves –

GENE Runes? What are you a fuckin' warlock!? This ain't the Middle Ages –

LULLABY Vandals and Visigoths –

GENE This is main street U.S. fuckin A. What the fuck you talkin' about Spider?

SPIDER Fine. You don't want to make the call don't make the call. I'll make the call myself. Just figured you could use the…the windfall.

GENE 'S that supposed to mean?

SPIDER You know, man hears things.

GENE Man hears things?

SPIDER On the street.

GENE On the street?

SPIDER On the street. In a bar. From a bookie. I got an ear you know.

GENE What d'you hear Vincent? Huh?

SPIDER You swim with sharks you liable to get bit.

GENE You heard I got bit?

SPIDER Swallowed whole, chewed up and spat back out.

GENE That's what you heard?

SPIDER That's what I heard.

GENE On the street.

SPIDER Jimmy's Bar and Grill.

GENE Jimmy's huh.

SPIDER 'Course I didn't put much stock in it at first.

GENE Why would you.

SPIDER Us being friends an' all.

GENE Brothers in arms.

SPIDER But that dice game out back. Boy. Them's some high rollers. Lose your shirt, they'll peel the skin right off your back too. They make your ex-old lady look like Mother Theresa.

GENE You heard I lost my shirt?

SPIDER The store too if it belonged to you. Guess it's just as well it don't.

> **LULLABY** *looks at* **GENE** – *this true? Takes* **GENE** *a moment to collect himself.*

> Fuckin' loansharks. Once they got their hooks into you, they got your number you know.

LULLABY What say Cap'n Gene?

> *Inside* **GENE** *is seething.*

SPIDER Listen I got to. There's this guy I gotta meet. OK I
leave the package here for safe keeping? Hour, couple
hours tops. I mean forget about the other thing. The
Mohawks. The res. The call. Forget it OK. OK. Forget
the whole thing. You're right. It's too risky. Just…trim
your sails. Hove to. Weigh anchor. Ride out the storm.

SPIDER *exits.*

LULLABY You know them Native Americans, the Mohawks
what have you. In their culture, you know what they say.
They say to want more than you need…that's a sure
sign a poor mental health.

Pause.

GENE *considers* **SPIDER***'s box sitting right there on the
counter.*

Pause.

*Then he grabs the phone, cradle and all, and emits a
primal cry as he readies himself to hurl it against the wall.*

Blackout.

End of Act I

ACT II

General Store – Later that night.

The place is empty. There's hammering on the front door.
GENE *appears from out back, crosses the store, arms*
himself with a snow shovel, and peeks through the blind
before shooting the internal bolt. **SPIDER** *enters.* **GENE**
whips the door shut behind him and locks it again. He
moves to a window and remains peeking out at the street.

SPIDER Jeez. Who put the bug up your ass?

GENE Ch ch ch.

> **SPIDER** *scans the counter for his box.*

SPIDER What?

GENE You see that GMC panel van across the street?

SPIDER *(absently)* What is this I spy with my little eye? What
panel van?

GENE The panel van. The cargo van. The black van 'cross
the street.

SPIDER DJ's Auto Repair?

GENE Not that one. The other one. The black one.

SPIDER The black one?

> *Finally* **SPIDER** *joins* **GENE** *at the window.*

GENE You see?

SPIDER *(pause)* I see a midnight blue GMC.

GENE Black, midnight blue, whatever. You see the van?

SPIDER 'Course I see the van. 'S parked right there under the street light. So what?

GENE So where the fuck you been that's what? Couple hours tops you said.

SPIDER And here I am.

GENE Dipping your wick in Peggy-Sue.

SPIDER Kaylee-Sue. And no –

GENE You can't keep your pants zipped five fuckin' minutes.

SPIDER I told you, I had some other affairs to attend to.

> **SPIDER** *scans the store.*

GENE Other affairs?

SPIDER Other matters of pressing business unrelated. Where's my package?

> **GENE** *looks out the window.*

GENE You know who that is over there?

SPIDER The box. Where's my box?

GENE You know who that is?

SPIDER I left it right here *(on)* the counter.

GENE I'm askin' you know who that is out there?

SPIDER Where's my goddamn box? Where's my goddamn bird?

GENE Will ya…jeez will you pipe the fuck down.

SPIDER Where's my goddamn golden eagle Gene?!

GENE I had Lullaby stow it out a harm's way.

SPIDER Stow it out of harm's way? And where might that be exactly?

GENE Good thing too. You know who that is in the van across the street?

SPIDER Scooby fuckin' Doo, how should I know!

GENE You been here this afternoon you'd know.

SPIDER Oh yeah?

GENE Yeah. Been out there since three. What's it now? Seven thirty. Eight?

SPIDER Quarter of nine.

GENE You see.

SPIDER What I don't see is that which belongs to me. What? You want a printed invitation to R.S.V.P.? Where the fuck is my goddamn bird?

GENE Safe. OK. Safe. And keep your damn voice down. All we know they got the place bugged.

SPIDER Bugged? What the fuck you talkin' about?

GENE That's what I been tryin' a tell ya. 'Cross the street –

SPIDER The panel van –

GENE The cargo van –

SPIDER The midnight blue van so –?

GENE U.S. Fish and Wildlife Service Office Law Enforcement.

SPIDER *(pause)* Go fuck yourself.

> **SPIDER** *moves to the door and peeks through the blind.*

GENE You don't believe me you sail across the lot go ask the man.

SPIDER How you know that's who it is? Could be, I don't know, anybody –

GENE Like who?

SPIDER Some contractor.

GENE Some contractor who?

SPIDER I don't know. The phone company. You wuz makin' all them complaints –

GENE The phone company. Then why's there no livery?

SPIDER UPS then –

GENE There's no livery –

SPIDER Gangbangers casin' the joint.

GENE Gangbangers? This neighborhood? What they gonna knock over the store steal ten bucks from the cash register.

SPIDER There's DJ's.

GENE Oh sure. He's got some real top a the line automobiles worth a boost. There's more rust in that workshop there is shop.

SPIDER Still don't make it the U.S. Fish and Wildlife –

GENE Man's been in.

SPIDER Man's been in?

GENE Here. Right here in the store. Stood standing right where you are now. Six one. Six two. Hun'red eighty pounds –

SPIDER What? You setting me up a blind date with your boyfriend. I give a shit he weighs in at?

GENE I'm just sayin' he weren't no slouch. Outdoorsy you know.

SPIDER So he's Grizzly Adams, so what?

GENE What I'm saying, I ain't seen the guy before.

SPIDER So you ain't seen the guy before.

GENE So every Tom, Dick and Harry lives within a thirty mile radius, them and their sister's grandmother's cousin, one time or another, they all set foot a the threshold.

SPIDER All stepped through the door huh.

GENE One time or 'nother.

SPIDER But not panel van man?

GENE Never laid eyes.

SPIDER Perfect stranger.

GENE Bingo.

Pause.

SPIDER So what's he say?

GENE Says he's just browsing.

SPIDER Just browsing? He's just browsing. Just browsing for what?

GENE Didn't say.

SPIDER He didn't say?

GENE Not specifically.

SPIDER He didn't say I'm an agent of the U.S. Fish and Wildlife Service Office and have you seen a goddamn golden eagle eight feet wingspan talons like Wolverine?

GENE Ch ch ch – I tell you the guy's not right.

SPIDER How so?

GENE Had him on a baseball cap. Thing on it you know. With a picture of a mallard. Says: Wild Goose Chase.

Pause.

SPIDER Wild Goose Chase? Mallard's a duck?

GENE Might not have been a mallard.

SPIDER Might not have been a mallard.

GENE Water fowl anyways.

SPIDER Wild Goose Chase. So what else?

GENE What else what?

SPIDER What else he say?

GENE What?

SPIDER He came in. He's just browsing. He what? He peruses the store. You say: Afternoon. Do you for something? He says what?

GENE That's just it he didn't say nothing.

SPIDER He must a said something?

GENE He was on a cell most a the time.

SPIDER On a cell. You catch anything? You hear what he was sayin'? You hear who he was talking to?

GENE He was mostly listening.

SPIDER Listening.

GENE Then he helps hisself a cup a coffee. Creamer. Buys a box a salt water taffy. Slides on out.

SPIDER A taffy man huh. So when was this again?

GENE I told you. This afternoon. Mid-afternoon. Around three.

SPIDER And he's been across the street ever since?

GENE That's what I'm saying.

Pause.

SPIDER He didn't see the package?

GENE Lullaby had already stowed it.

SPIDER Good.

Pause.

On a cell huh?

GENE And you ever try to get a signal this zip code?

SPIDER You figure he was play acting just to scope the place out?

GENE I don't know what he was doing, but I know it didn't sit right.

Pause.

SPIDER Someone should go over there.

GENE To the guy.

SPIDER Yes to the guy.

GENE And then what?

SPIDER And then...see if he makes a move.

GENE A move?

SPIDER Does he got a badge. Does he got a piece. Does he got a partner holed up in there.

GENE A partner –

SPIDER Reinforcements –

GENE Riding shotgun –

SPIDER Exactly.

Pause.

GENE So you mean to force the issue.

SPIDER Element a surprise.

GENE And then what?

SPIDER And then what? They do jump Louis we hightail it out the back a the store.

GENE You're saying Lullaby should be the one to –?

SPIDER To check the coast is clear. Hell yeah.

GENE How you figure?

SPIDER It's his store right. It's his neck on the block anyways, he got an illegal bird in here. No sense everyone gets burned.

GENE *(pause)* No.

SPIDER No?

GENE No I ain't sending Louis out there.

SPIDER Why the fuck not? You know he'd do it your say so.

GENE That's why I ain't sayin' so.

SPIDER C'mon Gene. He'd take a bullet for you. This is no time to let sentiment mess with ya business acumen.

GENE Forget it.

SPIDER 'Sides, he's *Lullaby Lou* right. How many guys he put to sleep that left hook. He can take care a himself –

GENE I said forget it.

SPIDER *(pause)* Fine. Then you go.

GENE Me? I'm not going.

SPIDER Well it ain't gonna be me.

GENE Why not?

SPIDER It was my idea. That's my…that's my contribution. I can't do it all. Carry you guys. There's got to be a division of labor amongst the crew. Parity.

GENE Parity?

SPIDER You think they let Eisenhower drive the first tank over the bridge?

  (off **GENE***'s look)* Hey I don't make the rules OK. I'm just saying.

  GENE *checks the street again.*

GENE Wait a sec. Whoa. Whoa. Whoa.

SPIDER What?

GENE There's a car slowing down alongside the van.

SPIDER Black n white?

GENE Tan sedan.

SPIDER Could still be a trooper. Plain-wrapper.

Long Pause.

So?

GENE Ch ch ch.

Pause.

SPIDER Gene?

GENE Ch ch ch.

Pause.

SPIDER So?

GENE Nothin. 'S just kids.

SPIDER Well all right. There you go. Maybe that's a sign.

GENE A sign? A sign a what?

SPIDER A sign our luck is changing.

Pause. **GENE** *remains at the window.*

GENE Thems Colorado plates?

SPIDER What?

GENE On the van. Thems Colorado plates?

SPIDER How the fuck should I know?

GENE Hard to see with the shadows, the angle and all, but
I think they're Colorado plates.

SPIDER So Goose Chase is a long ways from home. So? So what?

GENE So the National Eagle Repository is in Commerce City Colorado.

SPIDER The National Eagle Repository?

GENE 'S where they keep all the dead eagles cold storage.

Pause.

SPIDER *(pointed)* Now how, the fuck, would you know that?

GENE 'Cause I made the call.

SPIDER You made the call?

GENE Said so didn't I.

SPIDER You made the call.

GENE Yes I did.

SPIDER *The* call?

GENE Yes.

SPIDER My call?

GENE Your call.

SPIDER The call to the res? The call to Waneek?

GENE Who else I'm calling Oprah fuckin' Winfrey.

SPIDER You made the call I'm not even present.

GENE You said to call. So I called.

SPIDER Well what's she say?

GENE She said the National Eagle Repository is in Commerce City Colorado and she gave me the number.

SPIDER What number?

GENE The number of the Repository.

SPIDER She gave you the number the –

GENE Yes.

SPIDER For you to call?

GENE That was her recommendation yes.

SPIDER To what end?

GENE To what end? To hand in the bird.

SPIDER Fuckin' Indians!

GENE Hey!

SPIDER Fuckin' lowlife scumbag motherfucking Indians!

GENE Hey!

SPIDER FUCK!

GENE HEY!

SPIDER OK. OK. I'm sorry. I know you're close. I'm sorry,
but you know, jeez. Jus' tryin to do Dances-With-Wolves
a favor here, and that's the thanks.

GENE Ain't Waneek's fault. Whole things locked down tight
as a duck's ass is all. 'S just like you said: only enrolled
members of Federally approved tribes can put in for
a permit for the FWS to approve 'em. Anyone else
caught in possession a carcasses, body parts, feathers…
even for religious purposes, they gonna face the full
force of the law.

(removes a scrap of paper from his pocket) Pursuant to the
Eagle Feather Law, Title fifty, Part twenty two of the
Code of Federal Regulations.

SPIDER She tell you all this?

GENE Yes she did.

SPIDER And you wrote it down?

GENE The last part so I didn't forget you started kicking
up a rumpus.

SPIDER *(pause)* 'S not like I was hunting the fucker. I din' shoot it out a the sky.

GENE Don't matter how you came upon it. They's fried by some high voltage power line, crocked by a cropduster, hit by a semi – you find one a these creatures you's legally obliged to call it in. National Eagle Repository scoops 'em up, bags and tags them – whole birds or even parts thereof.

SPIDER Fuck.

GENE That's right.

SPIDER Fuckety. Fuckety. Fuckety. Fuck.

GENE Name that tune.

>   **SPIDER** *paces. Thinks.*

SPIDER *(pause)* How come the Mohawks ain't approved by the Feds?

GENE Who said they ain't approved?

SPIDER They approved what's the problem?

GENE Waneek says it's too big a risk.

SPIDER Oh she does?

GENE That's right.

SPIDER Like someone is gonna know one dead bird's butt from another?

GENE What?

SPIDER They ain't got VIN numbers tattooed on their ass. Who's gonna know where they got the turkey from once it's diced up into bite sized chunks?

GENE You're talking one bird. Waneek is talking multiple applications 'cross the whole tribe cross who knows how many generations. 'Sides, it violates the sanctity of her beliefs.

SPIDER *studies* GENE.

SPIDER You trying to pull a fast one on me Gene? Huh? You tryin' to pull my chain? You and that dumbass sidekick a yours? Where is he anyways? Huh? You two trying' to pull a fast one. 'Cause I will... I will... I will not take kindly to that my friend. I will...heads will roll.

SPIDER *looks around for a weapon. He takes a ladle from a display of kitchen utensils and wields it like a club.*

You un'erstand? Blood will be spilled. Do not test me on this.

GENE What? You gonna beat me to death with a spoon?

On 'spoon' a trapdoor in the floor behind SPIDER *opens with a crash.* SPIDER *reacts as* LULLABY *pops his head up from the basement. They lock eyes and both freeze for a moment.*

LULLABY *(re the ladle)* List price for the Twissler Magic Soup Ladle is twenty eight ninety nine. That's pure stainless steel.

SPIDER Get the fuck out of there.

LULLABY *climbs out and flips the trapdoor shut.*

What you doing down there?

LULLABY Opening a window.

SPIDER Opening a window.

GENE Look Ricky –

SPIDER DON'T YOU LOOK RICKY ME! DON'T YOU DO THAT!

(to LULLABY *re the trapdoor)* WHAT'S GOING ON DOWN THERE? HUH?! WHAT THE FUCK YOU DOING DOWN THERE?!

GENE *(re the trapdoor)* 'S where 'Erik's' at.

SPIDER Erik? Who the fuck is Erik?

> LULLABY *flaps his arms, mimes a beak and talons.*

> The ea...you mean the eagle!?

GENE *(indicating the place might be bugged)* Ch Ch Ch –

SPIDER Erik. That's... OK. OK. So that's...down there... down there is where 'Erik' is at?

LULLABY Uh-hu.

SPIDER And how is he? How is Erik?

GENE How is he?

LULLABY Deceased is how he is.

SPIDER But I mean, you know, he's safe and sound.

GENE Safe and sound. Snug as a bug.

LULLABY Really startin' to honk.

GENE Like ripe cheese.

LULLABY 'S why I opened a window the crawl space.

GENE That was good thinking Louis. Otherwise, Goose Chase comes back in, all he gots to do is follow his nose.

> SPIDER *sets down the ladle.*

SPIDER What is going on here? What exactly is going on here?

GENE I told you. The U.S –

SPIDER Yeah, yeah, yeah, the U.S. Fish and fuckin' Wildlife SWAT team raided the joint. You schmucks think I was born yesterday. You think I'm just off the boat. Huh? I'm gone what, couple hours, and all of a sudden the place is under surveillance? How they find it so quick? Huh? Answer me that?

GENE How should I know. GPS. A tag somekind.

SPIDER What?

GENE These are rare and sought after specimens right. Right. Goes without saying they might, you know, monitor flight paths whatnot –

LULLABY Breeding grounds, migratory pattens, nesting sites –

GENE ...so forth. For their, you know, their database.

SPIDER *(pause)* You see a tag on the...on <u>Erik's</u> foot?

GENE On Erik's foot, no.

SPIDER No? You didn't see no tag?

GENE On Erik's foot, no.

SPIDER Neither foot?

GENE No.

SPIDER Louis?

LULLABY Can't say that I did 'cause I didn't.

SPIDER Not the right, not the left?

LULLABY Din see no tag Erik's foot.

SPIDER How about a collar? You see Erik sporting a collar?

GENE They got chips.

SPIDER Huh?

LULLABY Microchips. Implants.

GENE My ex-ball n chain, she's got one of those little pooches. You know them little dogs size of a booger –

LULLABY You mean like a Chihuahua?

GENE I mean a Brussels Griffon.

LULLABY Never seen me a Brussels Griffon?

GENE Pipsqueak dog. Sprout. Stupid mutt. Cute as all hell, but not two brain cells to rub together.

SPIDER An' I should give a shit because?

GENE I'm saying he's all chipped up. Run a scanner upside Sprout's noggin, 's like a barcode on a pound a ground beef at the Pay Less checkout.

SPIDER How you know for sure?

GENE I got to pay for the sonofabitch.

SPIDER Not the...not the damn dog for chrissakes –

GENE Wanna get rich quick open a poodle parlor –

SPIDER I'm talkin' about the ea... Erik. Erik. How you know for sure Erik's been chipped?

GENE I don't. I'm speculating. But you ask me how come Erik's friends got wind of his whereabouts so damn quick, I don't know what else to tell ya. 'Cept maybe less someone saw you...you know...someone see you out on the highway pick up your *traveling companion.*

SPIDER No-one saw me.

LULLABY Erik hitchin' a ride –

SPIDER No-one saw me –

GENE You got Boz Scaggs on the radio –

SPIDER Boz Scaggs and then boom!

GENE And then what?

SPIDER And then what what?

GENE What d'you do exactly? Walk us through it. Talk us through your movements.

SPIDER What are you Columbo, this an episode a CSI?

GENE Just sayin' it might help ta...ta get a handle on this situation; a way out a this fix.

SPIDER   What? I …the eag… I meet Erik on the road. I eh… I pull over the hard shoulder. I gather him up…help him into the trunk.

GENE   Where d'you get the carton?

SPIDER   The carton?

GENE   The carton. The box. What you had it in the rambler?

SPIDER   No.

GENE   Then where d'you get the carton? Time you showed up here you had the ea… Erik…all trussed up like a Thanksgiving turkey ready to Fed-X.

LULLABY   Ready to UPS. Pickups 'fore eight thirty, A of the M –

SPIDER   The dumpsters out back of the strip mall.

GENE   Where?

SPIDER   You know, Rainbow Falls.

GENE   Which store?

SPIDER   What difference does it make which store?

GENE   I don't know. It might.

SPIDER   Popsicle Toes.

GENE   The ice-cream parlor there.

SPIDER   'Xactly.

LULLABY   'S good ice-cream.

GENE   Yes it is.

LULLABY   I like it.

GENE   What's not to like. Five bucks a double scoop waffle cone.

LULLABY   Ever tasted the kit-kat special? Made from real kit-kats.

GENE Good huh?

LULLABY Tastes like kit-kats.

GENE Uh-hu. You try the maple, walnut and Oreo mint?

LULLABY Always go for the kit-kat special.

GENE Next time you try the Oreo mint.

LULLABY Does it taste like kit-kats?

> **SPIDER** *moves back to the door, peeks out through the blind.*

GENE So. You go in?

SPIDER What?

GENE Popsicle Toes. You go in?

SPIDER Go in. No. They was closed.

LULLABY Summer thru winter don't open 'til noon.

GENE They know you there?

SPIDER I dunno. Maybe.

GENE You must know do they know you there.

SPIDER I've frequented the establishment on occasion.

GENE Then they know you.

SPIDER So they know me.

GENE So you're out back of Popsicle Toes. You got our friend in the trunk. You go through a dumpster find a carton. You make the switch right there in the parking lot?

SPIDER Yeah. And no – nobody saw me.

GENE 'S far as we know.

SPIDER 'S far as we know and that's very very far.

GENE Could be CCTV.

LULLABY Could be CCTV.

SPIDER I din see no cameras.

GENE Goes without sayin' there's cameras. Security.

LULLABY Goes without saying.

SPIDER Do you got cameras out back a this store?

GENE No.

SPIDER Well there you are then.

GENE We ain't the mall.

LULLABY No sir we ain't.

SPIDER I din see no cameras OK.

GENE But did they see you? That's the question before the court.

LULLABY A jury of your peers.

Pause.

SPIDER Look. Fuck. Nobody saw me. OK. So, here's the thing. If that's a U.S. Fish and Wildlife Service Office of Law Enforcement vehicle, how come it's so beat up?

GENE What?

SPIDER Midnight blue panel van. How come it's so beat up? Heap a shit.

GENE Undercover ops.

SPIDER And if he's been in the store and knows the whereabouts of our –

GENE Mutual friend –

SPIDER Our mutual friend. How come he didn't bust your ass already?

GENE *(pause)* Maybe he's waiting on a Federal warrant to search the premises.

LULLABY Maybe he's waitin' on backup –

GENE Or maybe he's seeing where this leads.

SPIDER Where this leads?

GENE You know, are we a part a some bigger ring, smuggling ill gotten gains around and about the place.

LULLABY State to state –

GENE 'Cross the border –

LULLABY Like Heisenberg and the Mexican Cartel.

Pause.

SPIDER 'Course there's another explanation entirely.

GENE 'S that?

SPIDER How Goose Chase got here so quick.

GENE What?

(aping **SPIDER***'s earlier jibe)* You want a printed invitation to R.S.V.P?

SPIDER Waneek dropped a dime on us.

GENE Don't even…don't even form those words your lips you un'erstand me –

LULLABY He formed 'em already –

GENE Just do not go there 'kay –

LULLABY He went there already –

GENE You give that whole line a reasoning a wide berth 'kay. A very wide berth.

SPIDER All right, all right, I'm just saying we gots to consider all the options here. All the ins and outs. All the variables. All the known unknowns and whathaveyou.

GENE Fuckin' drop a dime.

SPIDER Jus' somethin' smells fishy is all.

LULLABY That'll be <u>Erik</u>.

Pause.

GENE Somebody dropped a dime. How we know it weren't Peggy-Sue. Huh? How we know that?

SPIDER It's Kaylee-Sue and she don't know nothing.

GENE Oh yeah? How about her husband huh?

SPIDER She ain't married!

GENE Her boyfriend then?

SPIDER Her boyfriend? Her boyfriend? She's with me!

GENE Oh yeah. She's hot as you say she is, you's just another grease spot yesterday's panties.

   SPIDER *grabs a hold of* **GENE** *and raises a fist.*

Oh you wanna take a pop at me. Go ahead.

   GENE *pushes* **SPIDER** *in the chest with both hands.*

SPIDER Don't push me Gene.

   GENE *pushes him again harder.*

I said don't push me Gene, Everything got limits. Even friendship you know.

   GENE *pushes him even harder.* **SPIDER** *whips out a handgun he has tucked in the back of his waistband.*

GENE What the fuck?

SPIDER Go ahead Gene. Push me again. Go right ahead. Push me again.

LULLABY That's death right there Cap'n Gene. Just like The Rime the Ancient Mariner –

GENE Since when you carrying a piece Spider?

SPIDER Since things escalated.

GENE What?

SPIDER I left here you didn't have the cojones to make the call. I figure I'm gonna have to go on out to the res myself cut a deal. You think I'm going on out there to trade with Mohawks nothin' but my dick in my hand.

GENE You bought the gun today?

SPIDER What if I did?

GENE Well that's jus' peachy perfect. Another bright spark knows somethin's going down. Who you buy from?

SPIDER What's it to you?

GENE Who you buy from? Trey?

SPIDER No.

GENE Rydell?

SPIDER Shot some eight ball a 'while back. Ain't sin him since.

GENE The hell you ain't. That's a Sat'day Night Special am I right? Jennings twenty two. Injection molded zinc alloy piece a shit. It's got to have been Rydell.

SPIDER Well that's where you'd be wrong genius. Got it from Ronnie Barracuda.

GENE Ronnie Barracuda! Jesus H Christ Spider are you nuts. Kid in school knows you don't go near his janky merchandise –

LULLABY Kid in school knows that –

GENE First time you pull the trigger that thing'll blow your hand off.

SPIDER You say.

GENE Well don't wave it around in here.

SPIDER Oh yeah.

GENE Stow it.

SPIDER Fuck you.

LULLABY Cap'n Gene said to put the piece away.

SPIDER And I said fuck the both of yous.

> **SPIDER** *levels the weapon at* **GENE**.

GENE You point a junk gun at me?

SPIDER I'd say that's a fair appraisal a where we at.

LULLABY The many men, so beautiful! And they all dead did lie: And a thousand thousand slimy things lived on –

SPIDER Shut up Louis.

LULLABY ...and so...did... I.

SPIDER I said to hold your tongue motherfucking retard!

> **SPIDER** *turns the gun on* **LULLABY**.

LULLABY I looked upon the rotting sea, And drew my eyes away; I looked upon the rotting deck, And there the dead men lay –

SPIDER Last chance. Cease and desist. Can that mumbo-jumbo voodoo shit.

GENE 'S a fuckin' seafaring poem you ignoramus. Samuel Taylor Coleridge. Lou used to recite it we was deep sea fishing.

> **SPIDER** *presses the muzzle of the gun to* **LULLABY***'s forehead.* **LULLABY** *sinks into a chair.*

SPIDER A seafaring poem? A seafaring poem? A little sea shanty, that's what it is? Well it's mutiny on the bounty now my friends. Man overboard –

GENE 'S okay Louis. Spider's just riled okay. He ain't gonna pull the trigger. He's not mad at you he's mad at me.

SPIDER You brought this on yourself Gene. You brought this on yourself and Louis.

LULLABY The self-same moment I could pray; And from my neck so free, The Albatross fell off, and sank like lead into the sea.

SPIDER *(to* **GENE***)* Okay Cap'n Hook. Empty the register.

GENE What?

SPIDER The register, the fucking register. Open it and give me the take.

GENE You're robbing the store now?

SPIDER What's it look like.

GENE Oh this is beautiful. I'm gonna remember this day. They gonna write colorful ballads about you Spider.

>   **GENE** *moves to the register.*

SPIDER An' I know you keep a wrecking bar un'er the counter Gene so don't even think about it.

>   **GENE** *takes cash from the register. Proffers it to* **SPIDER**. *Finally* **SPIDER** *takes the gun from* **LULLABY***'s head.*

That's it?

GENE Twen'y three dollars sixteen cents.

SPIDER That's all of it?

GENE Slow day on account a we been closed on account a some birdbrained knucklehead got ideas above his station.

SPIDER Some going concern you inherited huh Louis. Some blue-chip stock you got here. You the new poster boy for the Fortune 500.

GENE So you got the register. Now get the fuck out.

SPIDER Not without my bird.

GENE You really stupid enough to march on out that door with a golden eagle in a box, man 'cross the street.

SPIDER You're right. That would be dumb. So no. I'm not doing it. Louis is. Goose Chase turns out to be who you say he is, that's your lookout. You and that skank Mohawk. You shoulda done the deal like I said, we would've all come out a this happy as clams. Now you got me backed into a corner. You pull in your line you got a Great White snagged on the hook. You best be careful he don't bite your head off.

(to Louis) Get me my fucking merchandise.

LULLABY *gets to his feet and sways like he's on a rolling sea.*

The phone rings.

Pause.

Well?

GENE Well?

SPIDER You expecting a call?

GENE May be the cops –

SPIDER Ain't the cops –

GENE Got the place surrounded –

SPIDER It ain't the cops –

LULLABY Arm yourself against woodlouse, termites, ants and roaches –

SPIDER Shut up Louis –

LULLABY ...and other annoying pests –

GENE How you know? How you know for sure it ain't the cops?

SPIDER Cops go in gangbusters, lights blazing, sirens screaming makes 'em feel safe.

LULLABY One hun'red percent effective both indoors and
out –

SPIDER I said shut the fuck up Louis!

(to **GENE***)* Will you pick up the goddamn phone.

GENE You pick up the goddamn phone.

SPIDER Ain't my place.

GENE Ain't my place either.

SPIDER Pissing contest Gene? Really. Last roll a the dice.

GENE You call it that.

SPIDER Whadda they call it back a Jimmy's Bar and Grill
huh Gene? What do *they* call it?

> **LULLABY** *moves to pick up the phone.* **SPIDER** *levels the
> gun and answers it himself.*

Lacy's 3rd and Main.

(pause) Yeah he's here.

(tossing the phone to **GENE***)* 'S the last a the Mohicans.

(to **LULLABY***)* Told you it weren't no cops.

GENE *(into phone)* Waneek?

> **SPIDER** *forces* **LULLABY** *into a seat beside the chess board.
> He sits opposite, keeps the gun trained on* **LULLABY**, *and*
> **GENE** *in his peripheral vision.*

SPIDER Tell her from me she can smoke my totem pole.
You tell her that Gene. You tell her the hell with the
chicken-shit Mohawks. I'm gonna do business with
some real warriors a the First Nation: the Shawnee, the
Chickasaw, might even throw the Cree a bone.

GENE *(into phone)* Uh-hu.

(pause)

Uh-hu.

(pause)

Uh-hu.

(pause)

When was this?

(pause)

SPIDER *takes a chess piece from the board and flicks it at* **LULLABY**. *He tosses another. Then another. Quietly enjoying the moment.*

Uh-hu.

(pause)

Uh-hu.

(pause)

Uh-hu.

(pause)

Yeah. OK. Thanks.

GENE *sets the phone down in its cradle and locks eyes with* **SPIDER**.

SPIDER So?

GENE So you hose down your Rambler Rick?

SPIDER I hose down the Rambler?

LULLABY Water water everywhere nor any drop to drink –

GENE Yeah. You mop up the blood on the hood?

SPIDER What d'you think?

GENE Windshield too?

SPIDER The windshield?

GENE Yeah. You clean the glass? We got some triple-A products here you wanna finish the job spic n span.

SPIDER You gettin' at Gene?

GENE Bits a bone, skin, plumage maybe trapped behind the wiper blades. Minor miracle it didn't bust the glass come to think of it.

SPIDER The fuck you talkin' about?

GENE You Rick. That's what I'm talkin' about. You barreling along the interstate bird the size *(of)* a Piper twin-prop decides to play chicken. Didn' even scratch the paint a your ride.

SPIDER Fuck you.

GENE 'Course we both know why don't we Spider.

SPIDER Boy that piece a feral tail has got you turned around. Filling your head with stuff and nonsense.

GENE Stuff and nonsense. How about a courtesy call shakedown from the poh-lice over at the res.

SPIDER Shakedown? What shakedown?

GENE Seems the Veterinary Clinic over on Westerly has put out an' all calls. Some stupid motherfucker broke in jacked a golden eagle from their holding pen. Bird was still alive last seen –

LULLABY Still alive last seen –

GENE And that was three days ago.

> *(pause)* You stupid, lyin' sonofabitch. That's how come no-one saw you out back a the strip mall. Popsicle Toes. You was never there.

SPIDER I was never there? They know me there!

GENE And no wonder the fucker stinks to high heaven; three days you didn't even think to put it on ice!

LULLABY Poor ol' Erik –

GENE A veterinary clinic. A fuckin' veterinary clinic. How you even know it was there Rick? Huh? C'mon. I'm dying to know. How you even know it was there? What, you went in to shampoo Peggy-Sue's merkin. 'S that what happened Spider? Or wait, no. Of course. They carry pharmaceuticals. Prescription meds right. You broke in to score some PCP.

LULLABY That's a horse tranquilizer –

GENE That it? You was after a little angel dust, caught sight of Erik flapping about in his cage.

LULLABY Poor ol' Erik –

GENE No. Wait a sec. That would credit you with a little imagination and we know you don't got that.

LULLABY Flappin' about his cage –

GENE I got it. I got it! Like I said you got no imagination, so the first part is true. You didn't make it up. You *saw it* happen. That's what happened. You're driving down the highway, some other Joe clips the golden eagle. *Bam!* –

LULLABY BAM!

GENE You go: *What the fuck was that man?!* You see the guy pull over. Feathers every which where –

LULLABY Theys flyin' on their own, floatin' on the breeze –

GENE Guy gets a hold a the bird. What, he toss a coat over it maybe? A blanket somekind? It's a beast you wouldn't get within ten feet of normal circumstances, tear your arm clean off.

LULLABY Bird a prey will hunt a wolf –

GENE But it's stunned from the impact right. So he stows it in his trunk. You're thinking *What? He gonna take it home toss it on the grill.*

LULLABY Side a pokeweed and cornbread –

GENE He's gatherin' those tail feathers off the blacktop, tells you the ins and outs of how theys a precious commodity. And being a good citizen an' all, he got to do the right thing and turn it in. And so. You. <u>Followed</u> him.

LULLABY *(pointed)* Yeeeah!

SPIDER *(pause; GENE has nailed it)* Oh so fuckin' what! You know. So fuckin' what. It's wing was fucked Gene. What's a bird gonna do it can't fly. I helped it out of its misery is all. A mercy killin' is what it was.

GENE A mercy killing?

SPIDER Yeah. And they can't trace it to me.

GENE You sure about that Spider? How you know? How you know a little bitty bit a blood didn't seep through the flaps a the carton stain the trunk liner.

SPIDER There ain't no blood in the trunk.

GENE You quite certain a that Mister Ragno.

SPIDER Fuck you.

GENE DNA my friend. They only need a tiny little speck –

LULLABY Tiny little speck of a speck –

GENE Invisible to the naked eye. Puts you smack back in the frame *whoever* walks out of here with the box. Rambler's registered to you.

Pause.

SPIDER I'll take my chances.

GENE It's a pretty picture sure enough. You in a pumpkin jump suit custody of the state. Kaylee-Sue littin out in your very own ride, top down, some cracker behind the wheel, her head buried in his lap.

SPIDER   Louis. I will not ask you again. GET ME MY FUCKIN' MERCHANDISE!

GENE   I'll do it.

    GENE starts for the trapdoor. **SPIDER** *cuts him off.*

SPIDER   NO! No! I want Louis here to do it! He's the captain of the ship now right? Right? Big fish little pond. With that comes a whole heap a responsibility. Time for him to step up and take hold a the wheel.

GENE   Ain't Louis' fault there's no dice on the deal.

SPIDER   I don't care.

GENE   Look maybe I can still set you up...ask around.

SPIDER   Forget it.

    (to Louis) Well what are you waitin' on man. All hands on deck. GET ME MY FUCKING BIRD!

    LULLABY *looks to* **GENE**. **GENE** *nods.* **LULLABY** *opens the trapdoor and disappears into the floor.*

    Goose Chase still 'cross the street?

    GENE *moves to the window.*

GENE   He's still there all right.

SPIDER   The van or the guy?

GENE   It's dark. Can't see the guy but the van's there for sure.

SPIDER   Well OK then.

    A pained shriek from the basement followed by sounds of a furious struggle and a crash.

    GENE *and* **SPIDER** *react.*

GENE   Louis. Louis you OK?

SPIDER   What the fuck?

GENE Louis?!

SPIDER Maybe it's the cops sneaking in from out back?

GENE Thought you said they went in gangbusters!

A tense pause.

Now the torn blood-spattered remains of his box flies out of the trapdoor giving **SPIDER** *a start. He's ready to empty a full chamber into it –*

SPIDER Where's my bird? Where's my fucking bird?!

LULLABY *appears holding his hand which is bleeding.*

WHERE'S MY MOTHERFUCKING BIRD!?

LULLABY He bit me.

SPIDER BIT YOU?! HOW COULD HE BITE YOU, THE FUCKER WAS STONE COLD DEAD!

LULLABY Not Erik! The raccoon!

SPIDER The raccoon. What fuckin' raccoon?!

GENE The raccoon?

LULLABY Bit my hand took off with Erik.

SPIDER WHAT?!

LULLABY BIT MY HAND TOOK OFF WITH ERIK!

SPIDER TOOK OFF? TOOK OFF WHERE?! 'S A FUCKIN' BASEMENT!

LULLABY Window in the crawl space.

SPIDER *scrambles down into the basement.* **GENE** *hurries across the store. He searches beneath the counter for a bottle of bourbon and a dishcloth. As he does so he sets a bunch of other items on the counter. These include a rogue tub of BOMB-D-BUG. He rushes back over to* **LULLABY** *and pours a slug of booze over his wound.*

GENE 'Kay champ? Now get on out the goings good.

LULLABY shakes his head. He's going nowhere. His eyes move to the BOMB-D-BUG on the counter.

Lullaby. You need to see a medic. So get on! Slip out the back.

LULLABY Is it he? Quoth one, Is this the man? By him who died on cross, with his cruel bow he laid full low the harmless Albatross.

GENE accepts LULLABY ain't going anywhere. Noises off from SPIDER hunting down the raccoon in the dark, cramped crawl space.

GENE flashes a glance at the trapdoor, then scurries back to the window to check the street. He doesn't see LULLABY cross to pick up the BOMB-D-BUG

GENE The Captain goes down with his ship is that it? OK Louis. You the skipper.

GENE sees the BOMB-D-BUG in LULLABY's hands. They share a look. GENE retrieves his wrecking bar from behind the counter. They move to the trapdoor.

LULLABY The spirit who bideth by himself in the land of mist and snow –

GENE shows his solidarity with LULLABY by picking up the verse.

GENE/LULLABY ...he loved the bird that loved the man who shot him with his bow.

Three gunshots ring out below.

GENE and LULLABY react. LULLABY pulls the tab on the BOMB-D-BUG to activate the fog. He tosses it into the crawl space and slams the trapdoor shut.

Pause.

Noises off - Spider choking.

GENE *and* **LULLABY** *lie in wait.*

SPIDER *throws open the trapdoor and emerges through a haze of Bomb-D-Bug fog. He still carries the handgun and clutches a single eagle feather. His eyes are stinging, he's blinded by the smoke. He waves the gun around searching for* **GENE**.

SPIDER You fuckers owe me the dollar amount a juvenile golden eagle! You hear me? Where are you?! Motherfucking raccoon! What kind of ship you running here Gene!? What kind a pox-laden vermin-infested scurvy sucking ship are you running here!?

Without warning, and in one beautiful fluid motion, **LULLABY** *grabs the junk gun and floors* **SPIDER** *with a perfectly weighted jab with his bloody bandaged hand.*

LULLABY 'S my pox-laden ship now you chawbacon yahoo and don't you forget it.

LULLABY levels the handgun at **SPIDER** *who lies unconscious on the floor. And it looks for all the world like he just might pull the trigger.*

GENE sets down his wrecking bar and approaches **LULLABY** *very cautiously.*

GENE The other was a softer voice, As soft as honey-dew: Quoth he, 'The man hath penance done, And penance more will do.'

GENE eases the gun from **LULLABY**'*s grip.*

GENE stands over **SPIDER**, *he recovers the stolen cash from his pocket and picks up the eagle feather.*

Pause.

A loud knocking on the door to the store. And it ain't the sound of knuckles, more like the weight of a nightstick. **GENE** *and* **LULLABY** *flash a glance at the locked door as the knocking grows more insistent.*

LULLABY Somebody knocking the door.

(pause) You tell who it is?

GENE I tell you who it ain't.

LULLABY Who?

GENE Erik.

Lights fade on the scene as the knocking continues into Blackout.

End of Play

ACKNOWLEDGMENTS

'The Address of General Washington To The People of The United States on his declining of the Presidency.' President George Washington, 1796.

'The Rime of the Ancyent Marinere' Samuel Taylor Coleridge. First edition Lyrical Ballads 1798.

FURNITURE & PROPERTY LIST

The action takes place in the interior of a General Store (a single static set) in a fictional small town in Massachusetts, New England. For the premier production, the store merchandise, and even the walls and furnishings were kept to a bare minimum: a ragged wall and counter made from dilapidated, reclaimed weatherboard; a wood burning stove with splits of firewood made from a garbage can; the nautical backstory hinted at with heavy ropes, hooks, vintage pulleys, chains, timber beams burlap sacks, two wooden (mismatched chairs) and fake blood. Using the natural hue of the old timbers as the basic colour palette, red, white and blue were then introduced as accents: A dull denim blue telephone, a blood red coffee pot and wrecking bar, off-white paper invoices on a spike. As each designer will bring their own ideas and inspiration to the piece, the following is intended to be instructive rather than prescriptive.

'Vintage' Cigar Store Native American (p1)

'Bomb-D-Bug' canisters (10 plus) (p1)

Telephone (old style rotary dial + spares for breakages) (p1)

Final Demand letters (p1)

A chess set (p1)

Two chairs (p1)

A stack of periodicals by a wood burning stove (p1)

Large cardboard box (+ spare) (p4)

Coffee Pot (the kind that sits on a wood burning stove) (p4)

Disposable Coffee Cups / Tin Mugs (p4)

Shoe Cloth (p6)

Periodicals (National Geographic / Time / Mother Jones etc) (p7)

Carton for the 'Bomb-D-Bug' product (p14)

Snow shovel (p35)

Scrap of paper (p45)

Stainless Steel Ladle & other kitchen utensils (p47)

Replica Jennings 22 handgun (non-firing) (p55)

Cash register (old school - circa 20th century) (p58)

US dollars and coins ($23 dollars and 16 cents) (p58)

Torn section of cardboard box (blood spattered) (p66)

Bottle of Bourbon (p66)

Dishcloths (p66)

Wrecking Bar (p67)

Bomb-D-Bug bottle on the counter (p67)

Imitation Golden Eagle Feather (p68)

(optional)

Vintage advertising signs (Coke, Texaco, etc)

Burlap sacks

Barrels/Wooden crates

Store supplies

Checkers Set & Board

Chalk Board

Oil lamps

Nautical style heavy ropes/pulleys/chains

SOUND/ EFFECTS

(off-stage sounds):

Garbage bins overturned (p18)

Rotary Dial telephone ring (p58)

Scuffle – Man vs Raccoon (p64)

Gun shot (handgun discharged in confined space) (p66)

Night Stick (knocking on wooden door) (p66)

LIGHTING

The play is set in the Fall, and the lighting should suggest a gritty, neo-noir, slightly heightened reality.

Blackout (p33)

Lights fade (p67)

Lightning Source UK Ltd.
Milton Keynes UK
UKOW06f2340210416

272746UK00001B/12/P

9 780573 132070